Manchester United

Kevin Brophy

Level 3

Retold by Michael and Judith Dean
Series Editors: Andy Hopkins and Jocelyn Potter

Pearson Education Limited
Edinburgh Gate, Harlow,
Essex CM20 2JE, England
and Associated Companies throughout the world.

ISBN-13: 978-0-582-43564-3
ISBN-10: 0-582-43564-1

First published 2001

3 5 7 9 10 8 6 4

Designed by Dan Newman/Perfect Bound Ltd
Printed in China
SWTC/03

Published by Pearson Education Limited in association with Penguin
Books Ltd, both companies being subsidiaries of Pearson Plc

Photograph acknowledgements:
Coloursport: pp 18, 19, 24 and 25; Corbis: pp 4, 15 and 27;
Popperfoto: p 17; Rex: pp 20 and 21; Photodisc: pp 34 and 35;
David Watts: pp 37, 39 and 40

For a complete list of titles available in the Penguin Readers series, please write to your local
Pearson Education office or to: Penguin Readers Marketing Department,
Pearson Education, Edinburgh Gate, Harlow, Essex CM20 2JE.

Contents

Introduction

The 45,000 Manchester United fans are quiet now. They have followed their team to Barcelona. Can they be three times lucky after their success in the League and the Cup? The score is still 1–0 to Bayern Munich . . .

History was made on that night in 1998. Only minutes from the end, United scored two goals to become Champions of Europe.

This book is the story of a great team: Manchester United are the biggest, richest and most successful football club in the world.

Kevin Brophy lives in Ireland. He spends most of his time writing, but he also teaches English as a foreign language. This is his first book for Penguin Readers. Some of his other books are *Almost Heaven, Walking the Line* and *In the Company of Wolves* (about football).

Kevin has one son and two daughters. His other interests are books and music, cinema and Wolverhampton Wanderers football club.

Are You a Manchester United Fan?

Choose the correct answers. Then try the questions again after you have finished the book.

1 **Manchester United's colours are**
  a blue and white
  b red, white and blue
  c red and white

2 **Manchester United's ground is**
  a Selhurst Park
  b Old Trafford
  c Maine Road

3 **Which team lost against Manchester United in the 1999 European Cup?**
  a Real Madrid
  b Benfica
  c Bayern Munich

4 **Who was a United manager?**
  a Matt Busby
  b Bill Shankly
  c Bobby Robson

5 **Which manager was *not* a Scotsman?**
  a Ron Atkinson
  b Matt Busby
  c Tommy Docherty

6 **Which United player was never sent off?**
  a George Best
  b Bobby Charlton
  c Eric Cantona

The answers are on page 41.

Three Times Champions!

'The 45,000 Manchester United fans are quiet now. They have followed their team to Barcelona. Can they be three times lucky after their success in the League and the Cup?* We are already in injury time and now they can only hope. The score is still 1–0 to Bayern Munich. The boys' heads are down, their legs are tired. A corner to United. Even Schmeichel has come up for it. Beckham takes the corner, the Germans get the ball away . . . no, there's Giggs! He kicks it towards the Bayern goal. He finds Sheringham . . . Goal! Goal! Sheringham has scored for United. One all, in the ninetieth minute. Let's see that goal again . . . The fans' hopes are still alive. Now, can Man U score again? There are only another forty-five seconds to play. Another corner! Beckham again, Sheringham passes to Solskjaer, Solskjaer heads the ball . . . It's there! It's in the back of the goal. This is unbelievable. Manchester United have scored two goals in the last seconds of the game. They will never forget 26 May, 1999. They have already won the FA Cup and the League, and now they have won the European Championship!'

---

* The League and the FA Cup: In the League, every team plays every other team twice, 'at home' and 'away'. In the FA Cup, a team only plays until it loses a game; the final is played at Wembley Stadium, in London.

SIMPLY THE BEST
Manchester United's historic win

The party in the streets of Barcelona did not finish until the early hours of Thursday morning. Manchester United made history in the Nou Camp Stadium last night with their 2–1 win over Bayern Munich.

The game was won in the final seconds by two goals scored by Sheringham and Solskjaer, both from corners by Beckham. Solskjaer, United's Norwegian striker, was on the pitch only eight minutes before he scored the winning goal.

Bayern Munich's Mario Basler scored the first goal for his team after only six minutes. The Germans were unlucky not to score again. They also defended well and turned away attacking balls from Andy Cole and Dwight Yorke. But in the end it was Manchester United's name on the Cup after the most exciting final of the European Championship in history.

The Nou Camp Stadium was completely full last night, with a crowd of 90,000 excited fans. About 45,000 Manchester United fans made the journey south. Many were wearing the club's red and white. Another 5,000 fans were watching the game at the Manchester United ground on Old Trafford's big television. Sixteen million watched the game on British television and about five hundred million people watched on television around the world, more than for any club game ever.

The party started immediately after the end of the game. The streets of Manchester were quiet and empty for ninety minutes, but then the fans poured on to the streets around Old Trafford. They sang 'We are the Champions'. They kissed, they danced. Even Manchester City fans, proud of their home town, joined the fun. 'Never seen anything like it,' said a red-shirted fan. 'The worst ninety minutes of my life and the best three.' Another happy fan said, 'We've done it. Ferguson is the greatest!'

United were the first English team to win the European Cup in 1968. Then they played Benfica of Portugal at Wembley Stadium and won 4–1. They had a Scottish manager then, too: Sir Matt Busby. Scottish managers have brought United luck. But today's Scotsman, manager Alex Ferguson, has taken United to the top. Manchester United have not lost any of their last thirty-three games. They have won three Cups in eleven days. As one fan said last night in Barcelona, 'It was the best night of my life.'

BOYS RETURN IN TRIUMPH

Everybody in Manchester stopped work yesterday when the triumphant United team brought the European Cup home.

A million fans came out to welcome the team. They sang and shouted and a few had tears in their eyes. United's open-top bus drove the twelve kilometres from the airport to the city centre.

One after another, the players held the Cup up. Irishmen Roy Keane and Denis Irwin. Ryan Giggs from Wales. Paul Scholes, Nicky Butt, Teddy Sheringham, Andy Cole, David Beckham and the Neville brothers, all from England. The Trinidad and Tobago striker Dwight Yorke. Ole Gunnar Solskjaer from Norway, Dutchman Jaap Stam, and Peter Schmeichel, the Danish goalkeeper who is leaving Man U tomorrow.

But the loudest shouts were for United's manager, Alex Ferguson. With three Cups in three weeks, he is the most successful manager in football. He is also the best Manchester United manager since Sir Matt Busby.

The fans think this is the greatest football team. The players think so too. They talked about the special spirit in the United team. Jaap Stam said, 'We have scored a lot of late goals at the end of games this season. We did it against Liverpool and we have done it here. I just think there is no better spirit than this.'

Ole Gunnar Solskjaer added: 'The team spirit is unbelievable. We are all in this together. That is why I stay in Manchester.'

The crowds stayed in the city centre until late in the evening. Everyone was wearing red and white; everyone was talking about Wednesday's game. Nobody will forget this night.

Perhaps we are a little sorry for Manchester City. But the City fans were keeping quiet. They were probably at the street party too.

Tactics

A 1960s team from Busby's time, playing 2–3–5

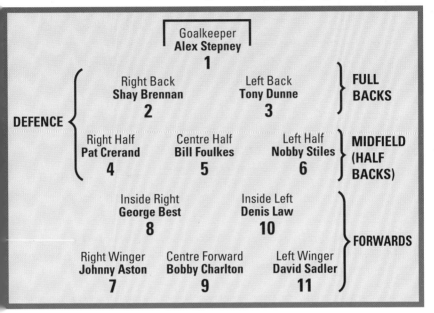

- The backs stayed near the goalkeeper. They played behind the wingers all the time.
- There was only one centre half.
- The same numbers always played against the same numbers in the other team: number 2 (the right back) always played against the other team's left winger, number 11. The right half and left half, numbers 4 and 6, always played against the other team's inside right and inside left (numbers 8 and 10). The number 5 (centre half) always played against the other team's centre forward.
- Tactics were usually the same in every game. The defence gave the ball to the inside forwards. The inside forwards passed to the wingers. The wingers kicked the ball – usually in the air – to the centre forward. And the centre forward scored! Usually with his head.

Tactics

A 1990s team from Ferguson's time, playing 4–2–4

Goalkeeper
Peter Schmeichel
1

Right Back	Centre Back	Centre Back	Left Back	
Gary Neville	**Ronny Johnson**	**Jaap Stam**	**Denis Irwin**	**DEFENCE**
2	**4**	**5**	**3**	

Midfield
Roy Keane
6

In the hole (midfield)
Eric Cantona
8

} **MIDFIELD**

Right Winger		Striker	Left Winger	
David Beckham	Striker	**Andy Cole**	**Ryan Giggs**	**FORWARDS**
7	**Dwight Yorke**	**9**	**11**	
	10			

- ✤ Man U's full backs do not stay back. They are very important attacking players. They give the ball to the wingers, and then they can run in front of the wingers. Gary Neville and David Beckham play very well together like this.
- ✤ There are two centre halves. They are often called 'centre backs' or 'stoppers' now.
- ✤ There are two centre forwards. They are usually called 'strikers' now.
- ✤ When the other team has the ball, all the players 'get behind the ball'. They move between the ball and their goal. *Everybody* defends!
- ✤ When Man U have the ball, everybody attacks. Everybody (except the goalkeeper) has to score goals. 'Defenders' like Neville and Irwin score a lot of very good goals.
- ✤ Tactics are different in every game. All the players play everywhere on the pitch.

Ups and Downs

The beginning

1878: Some railway workers in the north-west of England form a football club. They call it Newton Heath. The players wear red, white and blue clothes.

Did You Know...?
After Newton Heath, they wanted to call the club Manchester Central or Manchester Celtic. Then they decided on Manchester United.

1892: The club joins the English Football League in Division One.

1894: The club loses a lot of games, and it goes down to Division Two. The team changes the club colours to green and gold for better luck.

1902: The club has no money, but it is saved by a Manchester businessman, John Davies. He puts a lot of money into the club. The name is changed to Manchester United. The new club colours are red and white. Ernest Mangnall is the new manager. The club returns to Division One in 1906.

1908: Manchester United are League Champions, and in 1909 they win the FA Cup for the first time. John Davies buys land at Old Trafford for a new stadium for his club. It costs £60,000. Man U lose the first game at Old Trafford; the score is 3–4 to Liverpool!

Between the wars

1921–5: Man U return to Division Two.

1931: The club again has no money. It is saved by another businessman, James Gibson.

1939–45: There is no football at Old Trafford during the Second World War.

1945: Scotsman Matt Busby becomes manager.

Matt Busby's golden years

1945: While they are rebuilding the ground at Old Trafford, Busby is rebuilding the team. He sends out scouts to find good young players. The young players are called 'Busby's Babes'.

1948: Man U play Blackpool in the FA Cup Final and win 4–2.

1952: League Champions (and 1956 and 1957).

1958: After a European Cup game in Yugoslavia, Man U's aeroplane crashes at Munich. Eight players are killed and Busby is badly injured. While Busby is in hospital, Jimmy Murphy is the manager. United's first game after Munich is only two weeks later.

Did You Know...?
Matt Busby's Manchester United paid Manchester City £5,000 each year from 1945–9 to use the Maine Road ground.

1960: Busby returns to his job at Old Trafford. His most famous young player is George Best. Best joins Man U at the age of seventeen.

1963: Five years after Munich, Man U win the FA Cup. They are First Division Champions in 1965, and again in 1967.

1968: Manchester United are the first English team to win the European Cup.

1969: Busby leaves Manchester United for the first time. He leaves again in 1971!

After Busby

1972–4: Tommy Docherty is Manchester United's third manager after Busby. His time there begins badly. Man U go down to Division Two, for the first time since 1938.

1975: Docherty's plans begin to work. Man U return to Division One.

1981: Ron Atkinson becomes the manager. Man U win the FA Cup in 1983 and are one of the top clubs.

Ferguson's successes

1986: Alex Ferguson becomes manager.

1989: Success returns to United. They win the FA Cup.

1991: They win 2–1 against Barcelona in the Cup Winners Cup.

1993: Eric Cantona is bought from Leeds. Man U win the League for the first time in twenty-six years.

1994: Man U win the Double (FA Cup and League) for the first time.

1996: Man U win the Double again!

1997: United win the League for the fourth time in five seasons.

1999: Manchester United win the FA Cup, League and European Cup. No other English team has ever done this before.

The Red and the Blue

Part 1

Munich: One Man's Story

Harry Gregg from Northern Ireland joined Manchester United in December 1957. At twenty-five years old, he was too old to be a Busby Babe. Busby needed a good goalkeeper and he bought Gregg from Doncaster Rovers.

Two months later, on 5 February, Gregg was in the team which played Red Star Belgrade in the European Cup. The score in Belgrade was 3–3. The team flew to Munich to join their plane to Manchester. Some other people from the club, some reporters and a few other passengers were on the aeroplane with the Man U players.

Because there was a problem with the second aeroplane, the passengers waited at Munich airport. Did they have to travel by bus to Holland and then by sea to England? But after two hours, the passengers returned to their seats on the plane. It was snowing. John Berry, one of United's forwards, said, 'We're going to die.' Gregg laughed, with the other players.

The plane began to move, but it never left the ground. It crashed. It went out of the airport, across a road and into a field. It was suddenly quiet and very dark on the plane. Then the passengers began to move – if they could move.

Harry Gregg pushed past Bert Whalley, a Manchester United trainer. Whalley was dead. Gregg kicked the side of the plane and got out on to the snowy field. 'Run!' shouted the pilot. He was also in the field. Then Gregg heard a crying child. He did not run, but went back into the plane. He pulled out a two-year-old girl. Then he pulled out her mother.

There was a danger of fire in the plane, but Gregg returned again. He found Man U's Dennis Viollet and Bobby Charlton, and pulled them out too.

Then he saw Matt Busby. Busby was lying on the ground in the snow. He was in pain, with injuries to his chest and legs. Jackie Blanchflower was lying near him, and Roger Byrne was lying on top of Blanchflower. He was dead.

The injured people were taken to hospital in Munich. Seven players – Geoff Bent, Roger Byrne, Eddie Colman, Mark Jones, David Pegg, Tommy Taylor and Liam Whelan, all between twenty-one and twenty-eight – were dead. Three other United men and seven reporters died too.

Young Duncan Edwards lived for fifteen days after the crash. Before he died, his last words were, 'What time is kick-off?'

The next Manchester United game was played on 19 February against Sheffield Wednesday. Two players, Bill Foulkes and Harry Gregg, travelled back from Munich and played in that game. United won 3–0.

Manchester United reached the FA Cup Final that year. They played against Bolton Wanderers. A year before Munich, when Bolton Wanderers won the Cup against United, Roger Byrne said, 'We'll be back next year'. They *were* back, but without Roger Byrne. He was killed at Munich.

Everybody in the country, except Bolton Wanderers fans, wanted United to win. But they lost 2–0.

Harry Gregg will always remember Munich, and his friends who died. But *nobody* can ever forget Munich. Matt Busby stayed in hospital in Munich for seventy-one days. John Berry ('We're going to die') did not die, but he did not play again.

Gregg played for United until 1966. He has met the little girl from the plane again. Forty years after the Munich airport accident, Vesna Lukic came to Manchester to remember the team of 1958.

The Great Players

Duncan Edwards (born 1936, died 1958)

Duncan Edwards was the best schoolboy player of his time. He was the best player in the 1958 Manchester United team. Some people think that there has never been a better English player. He was in United's Youth Team and did all the usual trainee jobs – he helped in the ground, he cleaned boots. On 4 April 1953 Matt Busby said, 'Get your boots on. You're playing against Cardiff City this afternoon.' Edwards was the youngest footballer in a Division One team. In 1955 Edwards became the youngest English international player when he played for

England. This was a record until Liverpool's Michael Owen played for England in 1998. Training is important today, but in the 1950s players just ran around the pitch four or five times. Not Edwards. He ran around the pitch ten times. He was a strong man and a good, fast runner. He usually played half back, but he was good in any position. Once, playing at centre forward for the England Under-23s, he scored six goals. He could do anything and everything with the ball. Manchester United always played better when he was in the team. When Edwards died from his injuries after the Munich crash, he was only twenty-one.

Bobby Charlton (born 1937)

Bobby Charlton comes from a footballing family. Three uncles played for Leeds United, another uncle was a Leicester City player, a cousin played for Newcastle United, and his older brother Jack became a Leeds United player. When Charlton was playing for England Schoolboys, about eighteen clubs wanted him. But he wanted to wear the Man U shirt.

He first played at Old Trafford in 1956. This was the beginning of seventeen years as a Man U player.

Charlton's injuries in the Munich air crash were not too serious. He was playing again for United just one month later. He also played for England for the first time in April that year.

Busby had to rebuild the United team after Munich, and Charlton was always there. First he played left wing, but he was happier in midfield. He was named footballer of the year in 1966, after England's success in the World Cup against Germany. The same year, he was named European Footballer of the Year. He was United's captain in their first European Cup triumph in 1968.

During his seventeen years at Man U, Bobby Charlton scored 199 goals. He was a fair player and he was never sent off the pitch. He still works for English and world football, and he watches United play as often as possible.

George Best (born 1946)

George Best was the bad boy of Manchester United, but fans remember his wonderful football. He could do everything: win the ball, run with it, score goals, help others to score. And he was handsome, too.

A United scout saw the young Best playing in his home town of Belfast. Best was only fifteen when he arrived in Manchester. He did not like being away from home and he returned to Northern Ireland after a few weeks. His father sent him back to Manchester and he first played in the team in 1963.

One success followed another. In 1966 he scored two goals against Benfica, when United won 5–1. The Portuguese called him 'El Beatle', because he had long hair like the Beatles. In 1968 Best was in the team against Benfica again, when he scored a goal in the European Cup Final. Best was the youngest European Footballer of the Year in 1968.

In 1967–8 he scored twenty-eight league goals. But this was the beginning of the end. In 1972–3 he scored only four times. Best had many interests outside football and he had many beautiful girlfriends. His life outside football was more interesting than training. Busby tried to keep him in the team. When Busby left, Best became more difficult. He played his last game for United on 1 January 1974.

Denis Law (born 1940)

When Scotsman Denis Law was fifteen, he joined Huddersfield Town. He had a problem with his right eye, but he could not wear glasses and play football at the same time. He played with one eye closed. So Huddersfield paid for him to go to hospital.

Law was thin, but very fit, and he headed the ball well. Busby wanted to buy him in 1956, but he had to wait five years before he could buy Law from the Italian club, Torino.

Law was a good buy. When he scored a goal, he always put his right arm up. Fans saw Law's right arm in the air thirty times in 1963–4. He was named European Footballer of the Year that year.

But Law was unlucky in 1968. He was in hospital and missed the triumphant European Cup Final. The next day, Busby brought the European Cup to Law's hospital bed.

When Tommy Docherty became United's manager, Law went to Manchester City. In the 1974 City game against United, he scored with the back of his foot. Law's goal sent his old club down to Division Two.

Eric Cantona
(born 1966)

Frenchman Eric Cantona
played for six French clubs
in the same number of years
before he signed for Leeds
United in 1992. The Leeds
fans loved him. They
shouted, 'Ooh aah Cantona!'
every time he played. But
Eric was unhappy there. Six
months later he moved to
Man U and the United fans
began to shout, 'Ooh aah
Cantona!' and call him 'The
King'.

Cantona, with his
wonderful football, became
a favourite with the fans,
and for the next five years
success returned to Old Trafford. In 1994 United won the Double
for the first time and Cantona was the first foreign Player of the
Year in England.

But Cantona was a difficult man. He became angry very quickly.
He was in trouble in 1995 when he kicked a
Crystal Palace fan. He had to stop
playing football for eight months, but
United fans continued to shout his
name. The manager, Alex
Ferguson, understood Cantona
and made him team captain.

Cantona left football in 1997
and has acted in a few films, but
he is still interested in Man U. He
watched the European Cup game
against Real Madrid in April 2000 and
after the game he talked to Man U fans
for an hour.

Did You Know...?
Manchester artist,
Michael Browne, painted
a picture of Cantona and
other United players called
'The Art of the Game'.
Cantona bought the
picture.

Ryan Giggs (born 1973)

Ryan Giggs signed schoolboy forms for Manchester United when he was fourteen-and-a-half years old. Since his first game for United in 1991, people have talked about Ryan Giggs in the same way that they talked about George Best: beautiful football, wonderful goals. Giggs is fast too. In 1995 he scored United's quickest goal after only fifteen seconds! In 1991 he was Wales's youngest player ever, when he played for them against Germany.

In the 1990s, he helped United to win two doubles and three championships.

David Beckham (born 1975)

Manchester United has fans everywhere. David Beckham, a Londoner, was a fan when he was a little boy. He always wore a United shirt. He signed for United as a schoolboy, when he was fourteen. Everybody knew that he was a great player then. He loved training and he practised for hours.

In 1996 Beckham scored an unforgettable goal. United were playing Wimbledon and Beckham kicked the ball from inside United's half, over the goalkeeper's head, and into the goal – about

sixty-eight metres. But many people also remember when Beckham kicked an Argentinian player in a World Cup game. Beckham was sent off the pitch and England lost.

Some fans love him, some hate him. But Ferguson knows a good footballer and Beckham is *very* good.

Beckham has a famous wife – Victoria Adams, 'Posh Spice' of the Spice Girls. Their pictures are always in the newspapers. He is perhaps the most famous young footballer of today.

The Red and the Blue

Part 2

23

The Managers

Matt Busby (manager 1945–69, 1970–71)

After the war, there were two big problems at Old Trafford. Nobody could play football on that ground and there were very few players. The first problem was easy. United played at Manchester City's ground, Maine Road. The second problem took time. Busby sent his scouts to streets in big cities and to sports clubs. They were looking for boys who could play football. This was the beginning of Busby's Babes, the famous team of the 1950s.

Managers then were usually not very interested in training. But Busby was an unusual man. He put on his sports clothes and trained with his footballers.

Sadly, Busby lost some of his best young players in the Munich air crash. He began again, looking for new young players. But he also bought players from other clubs. Success followed. United won the First Division twice, the FA Cup and the European Cup.

Tommy Docherty (manager 1972–7)

Tommy Docherty, another Scotsman, was a different kind of manager. They called him 'The Doc' and he was like a doctor. He sometimes gave bad-tasting medicine to the players.

By the 1970s, United was a rich club. The Doc could spend a lot of money on successful players. He sold the older United players and bought good, young footballers. For example, he bought George Graham from Arsenal. Graham was the first of nine Scottish players who were bought by Docherty.

At first there were problems. United went down to Division Two. 'We'll be back,' Docherty promised. The next year United were in Division One again.

The Doc's biggest success was the 1977 FA Cup. He lost his job two weeks later, when he left his wife for another woman.

Ron Atkinson (manager 1981–6)

Ron Atkinson is a big, loud man from Liverpool, the opposite of quiet Matt Busby. He wears a lot of gold rings and people call him 'Big Ron'.

He was manager of a smaller club, West Bromwich Albion, before 1981, but at Manchester he began to spend money. He bought 24-year-old Bryan Robson from West Brom. for one and a half million pounds – a record for the next six years. Robson was expensive, but he was a great footballer. He was made captain of Man U in 1982 and he was also captain of England sixty-five times.

Big Ron liked to train with his team. He understood football and footballers. United won the FA Cup in 1983 and again in 1985. But Big Ron was unlucky. Liverpool was the winning League team five times. After some bad results in 1986, Big Ron left United and returned to West Bromwich Albion.

Alex Ferguson (manager 1986–)

Aberdeen was a very successful team in the Scottish League when Alex Ferguson was manager. He left Aberdeen for Manchester United when Big Ron left. Under Busby's management, United had a good youth training programme. Ferguson wanted to continue this and make it bigger. He wanted more scouts, more young players, more training. Success did not come immediately. But look at the Manchester United players who have come from the youth training programme:

A Manchester United Youth Team

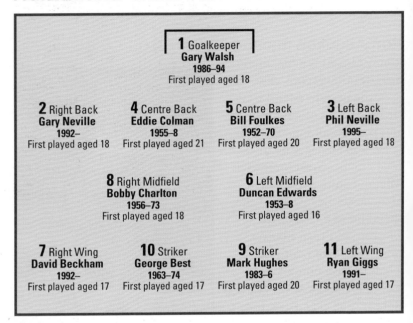

1 Goalkeeper
Gary Walsh
1986–94
First played aged 18

2 Right Back
Gary Neville
1992–
First played aged 18

4 Centre Back
Eddie Colman
1955–8
First played aged 21

5 Centre Back
Bill Foulkes
1952–70
First played aged 20

3 Left Back
Phil Neville
1995–
First played aged 18

8 Right Midfield
Bobby Charlton
1956–73
First played aged 18

6 Left Midfield
Duncan Edwards
1953–8
First played aged 16

7 Right Wing
David Beckham
1992–
First played aged 17

10 Striker
George Best
1963–74
First played aged 17

9 Striker
Mark Hughes
1983–6
First played aged 20

11 Left Wing
Ryan Giggs
1991–
First played aged 17

Ferguson is *always* looking for young players. If they are really good, they can play in the first team. But at first, only once! David Beckham first played for United in 1992. Then he waited until 1994 before he played in the first team again. He scored a goal against Galatasaray in a European Cup game.

Ferguson keeps his young players 'hungry' to play. Sometimes they train with the first team for two or three days. Then for two weeks they do their training with the Youth Team again. They never know if Ferguson is watching. He is looking for good football, but also for hard work, in training and in games.

Managers usually sell players when they are getting old and 'past their best'. Ferguson often sells players before that. When a player is playing very well, the price for him is high. For example, Ferguson bought 21-year-old Paul Ince from West Ham United for about two million pounds in 1989. Ince became an excellent midfield player and he was made England captain against the United States in 1993. But in 1995 Ferguson sold him to Inter Milan. Ferguson had three very good midfielders – Ince, Butt and Keane – so he could sell one. The price was seven million pounds, a record for United.

But Man U buy players too. A favourite United forward, Mark Hughes, was sold to Barcelona by Ron Atkinson in 1986. In July 1988 Ferguson bought him back at a lower price. The fans were very happy to have their favourite at Old Trafford again.

Under Ferguson, Manchester United pay a lot of money for the right players. Ferguson noticed Andy Cole at Newcastle United. There, he scored forty-one goals in a season. Ferguson paid six and a quarter million pounds for him in 1995. Dwight Yorke cost more than twelve and a half million pounds from Aston Villa in 1998 – a club record at the time. He scored two goals in his first game at Old Trafford and he has scored more than twenty goals every season since then. Ferguson's 'big money' strikers have been a big success.

Ferguson's players know that they have to work hard. If they do not do their best all the time, Ferguson does not put them in the team. There is always another player who is waiting to put on the red United shirt.

Did You Know...?

Man U does not only make money from football. It has a big shop where you can buy shirts. The club also sells Manchester United pizzas to fans.

The Red and the Blue _{Part 3}

29

Training and Food

The English football season starts in August and finishes in May. The training season starts in early June and continues for eleven months.

Manchester United's main training ground is The Cliff. The players train there five or six days a week. They usually begin at half-past ten in the morning and train for two hours, then for another hour after lunch.

The first week of training in July is mostly running and ball work. During a ninety-minute game, a footballer sometimes runs about ten kilometres, but footballers do not run for every minute of the game and they do not always run fast. The training run practises this.

The players run 100 metres quite slowly, but then they run faster, and then very fast. They repeat this running exercise many times.

There are a lot of ballwork exercises. Sometimes one defender plays one attacker. The attacker tries to get the ball past the defender. The defender tries to stop him and to get the ball.

In another exercise, each player has a ball and tries to keep it up in the air for as long as possible. He can use his feet, head, chest and knees. Sometimes the player passes the ball to the other player, but it must not touch the ground.

The players also use exercise bicycles, weight training, press-ups, step-ups and other exercises to make them strong.

In the second week of July, they play football games and practise tactics. The players practise free kicks, and the goalkeeper has catching exercises. At the end of July, they play five or six friendly games against other clubs.

They do not train so much during the season – usually for two hours, not three. Before a game, the manager and trainer have watched the other club. They discuss special tactics for the game and practise them. After a game, the manager, trainer and players watch a video of the game. If a player has not played well, he has to practise his weak points.

Food is important for footballers' health. In the past, footballers ate a lot of meat, potatoes, bread and butter. Today we know that the amount of body fat is important. Ryan Giggs has low body fat of about 8%, but 10–15% body fat is all right for big defenders like Jaap Stam, Ronny Johnson and Henning Berg. So the players eat healthy food. There is a restaurant at The Cliff where they eat lunch.

Here are two menus, one from Tommy Docherty's time at Old Trafford (the 1970s) and one from today. Which is the old menu? And which is today's?

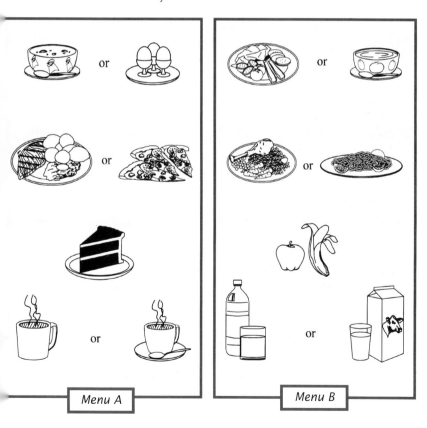

Menu A

Menu B

33

Fans Around the World

One hundred and forty thousand fans pay to be in the main Manchester United Club. But there are another 200 Man U fan clubs in Britain and there are fan clubs in twenty-four other countries. One of the biggest clubs has 28,000 fans in it and it is in Scandinavia!

Not all these fans can go to games, but many watch on television and video. Here are a few of the fans:

One day I'll visit Old Trafford. It is my dream. Keep winning, Man U!
Arene Magnussen, Keflavik, Iceland

In Singapore it is difficult to see Man U. The different time in England means we have problems watching games on TV. But your fans in Singapore think you are great!
Arif Amin, Singapore

I have been a Man U fan since Cantona played for you. I am still a fan now.
Cecile Lavanchy, Lille, France

My brother Wayne and I are fans. Wayne's dog is called Giggsy. I'm getting a baby dog soon. I'm going to call it Fergie. We are a Man U family!
Paul Feyrer, Detroit, USA

When I was on holiday in England, my parents took me to Old Trafford. It was the best day of my life.
Willem Kriek, Durban, South Africa

I saw Peter Schmeichel when he was playing for Denmark against Greece in 1998. He signed my programme for me. I'm proud that he played for Man U in the European Cup. Man U is my favourite English club.
Kostas Marcou, Athens, Greece

I had to stay up until five in the morning to see the European Cup Final on Australian TV. I was tired at school next day!
Greg Rinstead, Sydney, Australia

Hundreds of fans from all over the world visit Old Trafford every year. There they can see everything about Manchester United's history: the early beginnings, the famous players, the fans. There are shirts, tickets, programmes and boots from the past. But, best of all, there are the Cups. United have won a lot of cups during the last 100 years and they are all there in a special room.

There is a floor at Old Trafford where there are computers. You can choose the best players from any time in the club's history and make a Dream Team. You can also watch a favourite game and speak into a microphone. You describe what is happening – just like on radio or television.

No visit to Old Trafford is complete without a visit to the shop. The Man U shop is very big and it sells everything for fans. You can buy footballs, shirts, sports bags, books and videos, of course. But for the real fans there are also red-and-white watches and clocks, toys, pens and pencils, towels and bed covers!

If you want more information, the address is: **Manchester United Football Club, Old Trafford, Manchester, M16 ORA, UK**. Or you can find the club on your computer, at: **www.manutd.com**. There you can leave messages for the club and for other fans. Here are some messages from fans around the world, and some messages from enemies!

Name: Toshi
From: Tokyo, Japan
I am nine years old. I want to be a Man U footballer. Is there a football school for Man U players? What can I do? I love Man U.

Name: Manchester City lover
From: Manchester
So you think you are the best! And you can't win at Maine Road! Remember the 3-1 score? City is best!

Name: Fergus
From: Eire
I was so sad when Man U lost, I forgot my girlfriend's birthday party. She doesn't want to see me again. Is there a Man U girl who will understand me?

Name: Max Hurkmans
From: Maasluis, Netherlands
Has anyone a ticket for the 23 March game? I will pay a good price.

Name: Man U fan
From: Salford
We want to wear the newest Man U shirt but you change the shirts so often. Why do you always change them just after Christmas when we have had our presents? It's so expensive for the fans.

Name: Daniella
From: Belgium
Please send me David Beckham's address and phone number.

The Boot Boys

Manchester United's Hopes for the Future

Our reporter Ben Skilbeck is talking to three youth trainees at Manchester United's training ground, The Cliff. Jason Appleby and Christian Ricks are seventeen, and Daniel McShane is just eighteen. What are their hopes, fears and dreams?

Ben Skilbeck: *Many young boys want to be footballers. How did you start? Jason, let's begin with you.*
Jason Appleby: Well, like a lot of boys, I've always wanted to be a footballer. I eat, drink and sleep football. I can't remember a time when I didn't play.
Daniel McShane: Oh yes! You could kick before you could walk, couldn't you?
JA: Well, that's what my mum says.

BS: *What about you, Daniel?*

DMc: I started playing at school. But I wasn't very good until I got taller. I wasn't very tall until I was about thirteen. Then I started to enjoy my football. I'm a goalkeeper. I was in my school's first team, then a Man U scout saw me.

Christian Ricks: I was watched by a scout, too, when I was playing in my school team.

BS: *Was he a scout for United? You're not from round here, are you?*

CR: No, I'm from Bristol. The first scout was looking for good schoolboy players for Bristol City. Then later, a Man U scout saw me. I signed a schoolboy form for Man U when I was fourteen.

BS: *What happened then?*

CR: Nothing, really. I stayed at home for another two years. I only came to Manchester when I was sixteen.

JA: Yes, I signed the form at fourteen, too, and started training at sixteen. You can't play too much when you're young. It's dangerous while you're still growing.

BS: *Do you still live at home, Jason?*

JA: Yes, I'm from Wilmslow. It's only down the road from Manchester, but I have to get up at six o'clock. My dad drives me to the ground and we start at about half-past eight.

BS: *Where do you live, Daniel? Are you still with your family?*

DMc: Not exactly. I'm from Southport and it's a bit far. I live with my uncle's family during the week and go home at the weekend.

CR: I live with a family in Manchester. I don't see my mum and dad very often. I miss them and my girlfriend, Emma.

BS: *Yes, I'm sure it's difficult. I think George Best went home to Belfast. But he came back to Manchester again – and the rest is history! Do you two boys have time for a girlfriend?*

DMc: I have time, but the girls don't like going out with trainees. We're always tired – and we don't earn much money.

JA: Girlfriends can wait! Football is more important.

BS: *OK, tell me, Daniel. What does a trainee do every day? Do you just play football?*

DMc: No! No, first we put everything on the team bus and we come to The Cliff. Our weight is checked every day . . .

CR: Yes, we mustn't eat too much.

DMc: Then we tell the trainers if we have any injury problems.

Then, at about ten o'clock, we do our training. You know, heading, passing, ball work. That sort of thing.

BS: *Do you do that all day?*

CR: No, we stop for lunch. Then my favourite bit of the day – I don't think! Cleaning boots.

JA: Yes, we clean everybody's boots – our boots, the first and second team's boots. It's a dirty job, but somebody has to do it.

CR: Yes, I know, but it's *every day!*

DMc: No, it isn't. We don't clean boots on Wednesdays.

BS: *Why? What happens on Wednesdays?*

JA: The worst day of the week. We go to college.

DMc: It's not so bad. I like it.

BS: *And what are you studying?*

JA: Nothing very interesting.

DMc: I'm doing business. It's quite interesting . . .

CR: I'm learning the business side of sport, too.

JA: I just want to play football.

DMc: Yes, but if you have a bad injury . . . What will you do if you can't play? You have to earn money. What can you do then?

BS: *Let's hope that doesn't happen. Now, Daniel, you're already eighteen. Tell me what's going to happen next.*

DMc: This is frightening! United will sign me in two weeks. But only if they think I'm a good player. If not – well, I don't know. I'll have to think again.

CR: Perhaps another club will sign you. Like Ryan Giggs. He was a trainee with Manchester City.

JA: Right!

CR: And then Man U signed him before City decided. And what about Ole Gunnar Solsjkaer? He was playing in Norway's Third Division when a Man U scout first saw him. You never know when a scout's in the crowd. There are always other football clubs.

JA: No, there aren't. For me there's only one club and that's Man U.

BS: *So what will you do, Jason, if United don't sign you?*

JA: They will sign me. I'm a trainee here for another year. I'll work every minute to play better and better. I'm going to succeed.

DMc: Oh yes, our Jason is hungry for success!

BS: *OK, boys. To finish . . . Tell me your favourite Man U players, past or present. Christian?*

CR: I don't have to think. It's Eric Cantona. He played wonderful football.

DMc: Because I'm a goalkeeper, I like Peter Schmeichel. When he was good, he was great.

JA: I choose David Beckham. He's my favourite.

BS: *Well, thank you, boys. We hope to see your names in the Man U team very soon. Good luck, all of you.*

Dream Team

	Goalkeeper **Peter Schmeichel**		
Right Back **Bryan Robson**	Centre Back **Duncan Edwards**	Centre Back **Billy Foulkes**	Left Back **Denis Irwin**
	Midfield **Eric Cantona**	Midfield **Roy Keane**	
Right Winger **George Best**	Striker **Bobby Charlton**	Striker **Denis Law**	Left Winger **Ryan Giggs**

✤ Peter Schmeichel: He was a goalkeeper *and* another defender.

✤ Bryan Robson: The most useful player ever. He could play anywhere.

✤ Duncan Edwards: He died at Munich. We can only imagine the greatness that was possible from him.

✤ Billy Foulkes: A sure-footed defender.

✤ Denis Irwin: The best left full back that Man U have ever had! He can pass, head and score goals.

✤ Eric Cantona: The greatest player in the world in the space just behind the strikers. He could win games with his passes.

✤ Roy Keane: A great captain who could score goals. He could change a game completely.

✤ George Best: Probably the second best footballer (after Pelé) that the world has ever seen.

✤ Bobby Charlton: A great player – and a great sportsman.

✤ Ryan Giggs: He can run at defenders and go past them to the left or the right.

✤ Denis Law: He could score goals with his head, right foot or left foot, when he was in the air or on the ground.

What is *your* Man U dream team?

Are You a Manchester United Fan?: *Answers*
1: c **2:** b **3:** c **4:** a **5:** a **6:** b

Activities

Pages 1–11
Before you read

1 Find the words in *italics* in your dictionary. They are all in the book.
Which word is correct here?

   a a first *division/league* club

   b to win the *champion/cup*

   c to *goal/score* for England

   d to *manage/injure* the club

   e a dangerously wet *pitch/stadium*

   f a terrible team *spirit/triumph*

   g a *fan/scout* for an important club

   h to learn new *tactics/records*

2 What do you think these parts of the book are about?

1 Three Times Champions	**a**	Manchester United, 1878–1999
2 Tactics	**b**	Manchester United, 1999
3 Ups and Downs	**c**	The great Manchester United teams of the past and now

After you read

3 Explain in your own words what happened on 26 May, 1999.

4 Read about the tactics on pages 7 and 8 again. Does your
favourite team use tactics like these? If not, how do they play?
How should they play?

Pages 12–27
Before you read

5 Answer these questions. Find the words in *italics* in your dictionary.

   a Who is the *captain* of your favourite football team?

   b How many *kick-offs* are there in a game that ends 1–1?

   c Why do footballers *train*?

   d What is a *youth* team?

6 Discuss what a manager or a scout looks for in young players.
What is most important, do you think?

After you read

7 Answer these questions.

  a Which of the footballers in *The Great Players* played longest for Man U?

  b Why did Man U fans call Cantona 'The King'? And why do you think the Leeds fans were angry?

  c How many English players finished the 1998 World Cup game against Argentina? Why?

  d What did Busby do that was unusual in the 1950s?

  e How does Ferguson keep his young players 'hungry'?

Pages 28 – 41

Before you read

8 What do you think is going to happen in *The Red and the Blue*? What do you want to happen?

After you read

9 Discuss these questions.

  a What kind of training makes footballers strong? What makes them fast?

  b Why do they not train so much during the season?

  c Why does Man U change its shirt so often?

  d Why must young players on the youth training programme go to college one day a week?

Writing

10 You are a Man U fan or a Bayern Munich fan in Barcelona for the 1999 European Cup Final. Write a postcard home the next morning.

11 Write a newspaper report about the Munich air crash.

12 Compare Duncan Edwards and George Best. How were they different?

13 You are the 'boot boy', Daniel McShane. Manchester United have signed you as a player. Write a letter home to tell your parents.

Answers for the Activities in this book are available from your local office or alternatively write to: Penguin Readers Marketing Department, Pearson Education, Edinburgh Gate, Harlow, Essex CM20 2JE.

BESTSELLING
PENGUIN READERS

AT LEVEL 3

Amistad

Braveheart

British Life

Dracula

Forrest Gump

The Horse Whisperer

K's First Case

Matilda

Princess Diana

Rain Man

Sense and Sensibility

The Thirty-nine Steps